TABLE OF C

INTRODUCTION 1
CRICUT EASYPRESS WITH IRON-ON VINYL 7
    DIY Iron-on Vinyl on Wood Design 7
    DIY a Banner with Iron-on Vinyl on Cardstock 9
    DIY Cricut Stencil Using A Stencil Blank 10
    DIY Stenciling Your Home Décor Design 13
OTHER CRICUT PROJECT 15
    Herringbone Themed Wall Anchors 15
    Customized Shoes 17
    Glasswork and Glass Etching 20
    Marbled Journal and Vinyl Art 23
    Customized Coffee Cups 25
PROJECTS FOR INTERMEDIATE 28
    Fabric Headband 28
    Forever Fabric Banner 29
    Fabric Flower Brooch 31
    Leather Flower Hat 32
    Floral Mousepad 33
    Jelly Bean Burp Cloth 34
    Personalized Coaster Tiles 36
DIY PROJECTS 38
    DIY Monogram Can Koozies 38
    Oogie Boogie Treat Packs 39
    Teacher Tumbler Blessing Thought 41

    Diy Magnet Chore Chart 42

    Diy Grinch Glasses 44

GIFT IDEAS 46

    Making a Baby Elephant for a Birthday Gift 46

    Customized Suede Diary 48

    Mr. and Mrs. Gift Mugs 51

    Christmas Sweet Jar 53

PROJECTS IDEAS WITH GLASS 56

    Etched Monogrammed Glass 56

    Live, Love, Laugh Glass Block 57

    Unicorn Wine Glass 59

PROJECT IDEAS AT HOME 62

    Flower Garden Tote Bag 62

    Wild OX Plaid No-Sew Reindeer Cushion 63

    Framed Succulents Made from Paper 65

    Wooden Hand Lettered Sign 66

    Hexie Hand Towels 68

    DIY Baby Milestone Blanket 70

SOME MORE IDEAS 73

    Pumpkin Pillows 73

    Burlaps 74

    Felt Banners 75

    Coffee Sleeves 76

    3D Butterfly Wall Art 78

CONCLUSION 84

INTRODUCTION

A breakthrough in the use of the Cricut machine happened when the tool was introduced to cut out shapes. The machine came with a number of different cutting plates that let you cut out various shapes, letters, hearts, etc. It is possible to cut out pieces of paper with vertical and horizontal lines, but it is much more practical to cut shapes. You can also create your own designs with the help of all the templates that are available. For example, you can use a template to create a 'Jelly Bean' design on fabric or paper. The templates are like stencils that can be used over and over again to create designs of every kind. You can also use chalk or crayons to draw patterns on paper or fabric. Once the pattern is drawn on paper or fabric, you can trace it while using the Cricut machine's cutting tool. You can also take pictures using your phone or camera and then use a template from the Cricut portfolio to cut the image out. The machine cuts patterns such as shapes, words, numbers, and designs that are precise enough for stitching. You can create paper designs but you can also create the same shape through embroidery on a piece of fabric. Another striking feature of this machine is its ability to cut out everyday objects like buttons, bottles, toys, etc. You can even cut out different shapes from a single piece of fabric which can be used for creating clutches or other fashion accessories. The company offers different models of Cricut machines for different kinds and sizes of projects that may be required by customers.

We are proud to introduce the Cricut® Project Special Decoration. Here are some of the functions of various cricut machines:

Cricut® Express:

The Express is a new machine which features a full-color LCD screen and a new die-cutting system. It has a built-in blade storage, but does not have a double-cut feature. It has 5,000 stitches per minute. It can cut up to 4" wide x 8" long and store up to ten cuts at a time. This machine can be used on standard and wide capacity spools. The Cricut Express is designed for card making, scrapbooking, tags, apparel and much more.

Cricut Designer® DT:

This new model is portable, easy to use and cuts up to 1/2" wide x 8" long with a blade that can cut through cardboard or foam core material (like an X-Acto). It can cut any project with up to 6" tall finished card size pieces. It has 1,000 stitches per minute and comes with one 32 pieces set of blades (which can be replaced) plus 5-piece accessory sets. It is specifically designed for jewelry making, scrapbooking, tags and apparel projects. The Cricut Designer uses the same high-quality blades that are found in our Cricut Express machines.

Cricut Maker® 3D:

The perfect machine for making unique gifts or cards! This new model cuts up to 1/4" thick material (cardboard, foam core or fabric). It features 3" LCD screen from which you can watch your project come together as it is being cut. The machine includes a blade storage tray for easy access to blades so you can always be ready to cut another project!

What is Cricut?

The name Cricut stands for "The Original Cutting Machine". It stands for the machines but it also stands for the company. The word "cricut" has come to mean "Cricut machine" in everyday language.

What is a Cricut Mini?

A "mini" version is a smaller version of the original "Original Cricut Machine". There are many, many versions of both the original Cricut machine and the Cricut Mini, but we call them ""mini" because they are really small. You can choose from different colors or designs and you will be happy with your selection.

What does it cut? Where does it cut? The cricut machine cuts lots of things, some people think of it as a cutting machine and some think of it as a paper crafting/scrapbooking machine because it's got that special ability to cut fabric, vinyl, cardstock and other materials. But the cricut can also make artistic cuts with material that you print or get from a computer program like Adobe® Illustrator®. You can cut in a special way with scrolls, swirls and patterns that look like they have been painted on paper. The cricut can also make very precise cuts like paper dolls or garments so you can cut out amazing hats, coats, shapes or dolls at home! The cricut mini allows you to cut through wood, plastic, foam and cardstock with the same ease as butter! It's really an all-in-one package!

Let's take a look at the Press. It's essentially a paper cutting machine although it can handle cardstock, tissue paper, and other materials. The depth of cut is variable and you can turn various settings on or off to best suit your needs. You can cut straight lines or curves, but the press also has an auto-level function that takes care of that automatically for you.

Cricut mini and cricut press are not magic tools. We have been doing this since 1999, so we have seen and used every type of tool available. I know every designer has their favorite, but there is always a reason for a designer to embrace cricut or other machines.

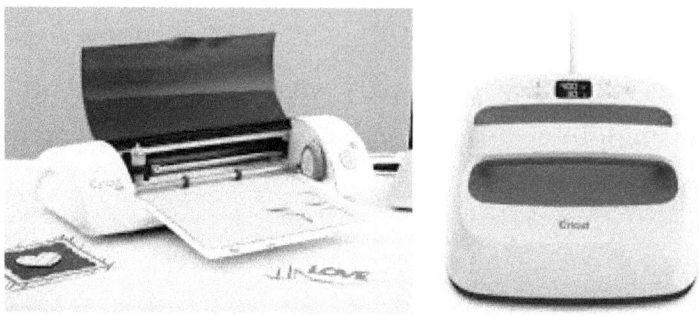

Cricut mini is best described as the workhorse of the Cricut family of machines. It is the most affordable machine in the line-up of the Cricut family. Because of its lower cost, it tends to be used for smaller projects, such as card making, scrapbooking, gift making and weaving.

Cricut mini can also be used to make more complicated projects such as table runners, placemats and waistbands. This machine is an excellent choice for beginners who want to get into one of these two advanced machines.

The cricut press is similar to cricut mini in many ways, with some exceptions. The major difference between the two is that cricut press has adjustable pressure settings that cricut mini does not have. This means that you can use this machine to make more advanced projects. Some would argue that this feature is vital when it comes time to create projects with intricate details from your imagination or designs from other designers. How many times have you looked at a design on the internet only to see it spread out and not look like what you had in mind? With cricut press you can take advantage of different styles of cutting without losing detail in your project because you have too much pressure on your tool.

Functions of Various Cricut Machines

The Cricut Machine is a fairly new machine compared to the Cricut Cutting Machine and Cricut Design Space. It can be used for many different materials including: custom stickers, cards, invitations, tags, and stationary. The Cricut Machine can also be used to cut vinyl.

Cricut Mini Press Type 2: The Cricut Mini Press Type 2 has the ability to print on standard business card stock or thicker stock (up to 12 inches). The Mini Press Type 2 is compatible with a wide variety of software including Dragon Maker® and Canvas Pro®.

Cricut Designer™: The Cricut Designer™ cuts 2x4 inch material for scrapbooking or other projects like gift tags. It is compatible with a variety of software including Dragon Maker® and Canvas Pro®. The machine uses standard plain paper as well as specialty card stock. The Cricut Designer™ will cut most materials including cardstock and cardboard. A special tool must be used for cutting through metal or fabric like acetate or hardwood.

Cricut Design Space™: This machine was released in May 2007 as a standard upgrade to the Cricut Expression™ and the Cricut Explore™. It features dual cutting points and a screen that provides more information about the design being created on the cutting mat. It can cut through most materials including cardstock, vinyl (in some cases), and paper.

CRICUT EASYPRESS WITH IRON-ON VINYL

DIY Iron-on Vinyl on Wood Design

The two types of vinyl—iron-on and adhesive vinyl can be used for wood design. Still, the iron-on vinyl is perfect for wood design because the wood surface is rough, and it takes a significant amount of effort before the vinyl stick to its cover of the wood.

However, iron-on tends to adhere perfectly to the wood surface, and you do not need a transfer tape because the vinyl complies entirely with the transfer sheet.

Supplies for wood design

- Iron-on vinyl
- Wood plaque
- Weeding tool
- Design Cricut space file
- Cricut EasyPress

Directions to create an iron-on wood design

1. The first step is to download the SVG file or create your preferred design on the Cricut Design Space.
2. Set the Cricut machine dial to iron-on.
3. Make sure you mirror the image.
4. Before you send the design to the machine to cut, endeavor to place the iron-on vinyl on the cutting mat.
5. Cut the file or design on your Cricut machine.
6. Once the Cricut machine is finished cutting, weed out the excess vinyl.

Hint

If you mirror your image in the Cricut design space, you will see that your image is backward, but when you flip it on the wood, it will show up the right way.

- The next step is to turn on your Cricut Easypress and set the dial to the right setting for wood on the vinyl project; the standard environment for the most wood project is 300 degrees and 40 seconds.
- Then firmly press down your Cricut EasyPress to the wood.

Hint

You can use a piece of cotton fabric between the Cricut EasyPress and the vinyl. This helps you to move the Cricut EasyPress around quickly, making sure you capture all the parts of your transfer design. Also, note that you can do additional press if the vinyl didn't adhere properly to the wood.

- Gently peel off the back plastic from the wood.

This is the process to take in adhering vinyl to wood, and you can use this technique for various projects relating to wood.

DIY a Banner with Iron-on Vinyl on Cardstock

Out of all the primary materials you can use iron-on vinyl with, paper and cardstock are the most inexpensive of them all—and you can create a beautiful project with them.

The following steps will show you how to use vinyl on cardstock by creating a banner that can be used for engagements, as gifts, weddings, and parties.

Supplies for Banner

- Cricut Easypress or household iron
- A white cardstock
- A gold glitter iron-on vinyl
- A ribbon

Directions of using iron-on on cardstock to create a banner

1. Download banner SVG cut file. And you can design your banner file or upload the downloaded file to Cricut Design Space.

Hint

Note that the banner file usually comes with a measurement of 5 inches x 7 inches, but you can resize it to your preference. Do not forget to mirror your iron-on vinyl so that your letters will face the right direction when you iron them to your cardstock or any other material.

- Once the Cricut machine has cut your cardstock and glitter iron, then you can weed out the negative area from the iron-on vinyl.
- Line up all the iron-on pieces over the cardstock pans. You can use household iron or Cricut EasyPress to press the vinyl to the cardstock.

Hint

For cardstock, low heat is required for adhesion. Press for a minimum of 30 seconds and flip to press for 15 seconds from the back.

1. Peel off the plastic liner after the heat press and keep the paper from curling by placing them under heavy object like a book.
2. Use ribbon to string together your newly made banner pieces.

DIY Cricut Stencil Using A Stencil Blank

When it comes to creating a Cricut stencil, there are different ways this can be achieved. However, this tutorial will dwell on how to cut a stencil with the Cricut Design Space.

Supplies for Cricut Stencil

- Stencil blank
- Paint tray
- A standard green grip or a standard purple grip
- A paintbrush
- Woodcraft frame
- Sponge brushes
- A transfer tapes

Directions for creating a Cricut Stencil

1. The first step is to make a stencil in Cricut Design Space.
2. Create a new project design from your Cricut Design Space. On the left side, click upload and navigate the design you created. Click "Save " to save the design.
3. The next step is to select the file you uploaded, and to bring it into your canvas, click "insert images."

Hint

You can always create your stencil design using the Cricut Design space instead of downloading from the SVG file.

- To start by creating your stencil file, click on shapes located on the left part of the Cricut design.
- Select your preferred shape for your stencil project.

- The next step is to resize the shape you chose to fit in the frame of the design text.

Hint

It is advisable to measure the shape to be half in size of the frame so that you will have room left when you tape your design to the backing board without a shift in space.

- The next step is to arrange your shape and image in good order by using the edit toolbar or align tools under the Arrange menu.
- What you are going to do is now to slice your stencil design. Click on the image and the shape of your stencil design and click "slice" located at the bottom of the layer panel.

Hint

Slicing is the process of splitting your stencil design into different layers until you are left with only your stencil piece.

- Click "Make It" to send the stencil piece to the Cricut machine for cutting. Then click continue to start the cutting process. Besides, on the "make screen," click on the browse all materials and select stencil.
- On your Cricut machine, set the dial to " Custom."
- Press the blinking "C" button to start cutting your stencil.

Hint

Before you try to eject the cutting mat from the machine, make sure your stencil is cut through the layering piece; if not, press the "C" button again. The machine will repeat the cutting process.

DIY Stenciling Your Home Décor Design

After you now have the stencil design you cut from the Cricut machine, you can now begin the home décor design.

- You start by taping your stencil inside your frame.

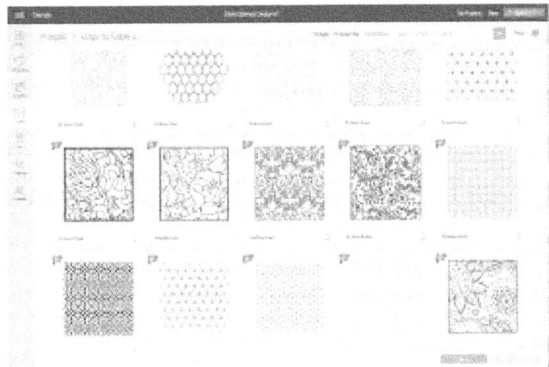

Hint

There are two primary options you can use to tape your stencil to the frame.

- The first option is to splash white paint all over the frame because the white background mix will give you a crispy line even though this is a risky option because the mixture of a white background with a different color can make your stencil to peel off when you pull it over.
- The next option is to splash a layer of mod podge on the same stencil. Both options are the same concept for taping, but the second option gives the same result in pulling up the stencil.

This tutorial will, however, focus on using a sponge with a small quantity of paint. Mix it inside a scratch paper and paint the stencil.

Hint

While painting, use a small amount of paint and do not use the brushing method to avoid bleeding all over your stencil, instead use the dabbing movement.

1. Continue with the dabbing movement in applying paint until all the stencil is covered.
2. The next step is to peel the tape and carefully pull up the stencil from the frame. But do this before the paint settles into the stencil.
3. Once it is dry, your stencil is ready for home décor. You can also use a poly coating if it's for artwork.
4. You can use this same tutorial to make various stencil designs.

OTHER CRICUT PROJECT

Herringbone Themed Wall Anchors

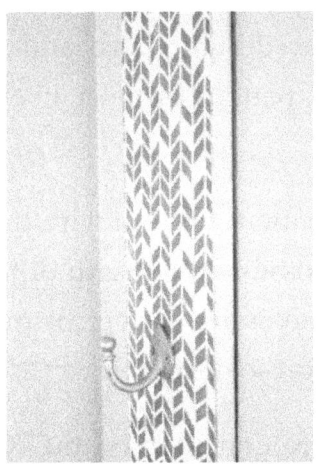

Materials:

- Cricut machine
- Vinyl
- Pine board (12" width)
- Hooks
- Wax
- Finish paint
- Drill
- Screws
- Foam brushes

Instructions:

- Sand, the pine board, then put on a coat of your favorite stains. Make use of foam then bush with a rag to apply it evenly.

- Go into your design space and get the herringbone design. This pattern is most likely available on your stencil.

- Design the pattern to fit in with the width of your pine board and possibly the length of the board if you want it to cover the entire surface or maybe just halfway or any length you so desire.

- When you are done, tap on the "GO" icon on the user interface from which you will proceed to the preview window.

- Go with the prompts that come up.

- Load up the vinyl and the mat.

- Ensure that the machine is set to vinyl.

- Tap on the GO button.

- After the cutting process is done, remove the cut material from the machine, and then place it on the pine board.

- Coat the cutting on the board with your choice of paint and allow it to dry.

- Remove the vinyl cutting and then sand it a little again.

- Wax the board, allow it to dry, and then use a lint-free cloth to buff it up.

- Get some anchors and place in the predrilled holes on the board before hanging it up on the wall.

Customized Shoes

Instructions:

- Canvas shoes in any color (we recommend white)

- Cricut Iron-on (colors of your choice)

- Cricut Easy Press (mini version would work the best) – you can also use a regular iron – small iron would be perfect

- Weeding tool

- Cricut machine

Materials:

- First you want to make sure that your patterns for shoes are ready and that you have canvas shoes to work with. You can download free patterns like sprinkles or animal prints that you can use on vinyl to customize the shoes. You can also make your own designs in Design Space. Make sure to arrange the line type to "Cut" when you are done with designing and before you send your design to cut. You can also browse through the Image library and search for suitable patterns there. Use the search bar to narrow down your searches and become more efficient.

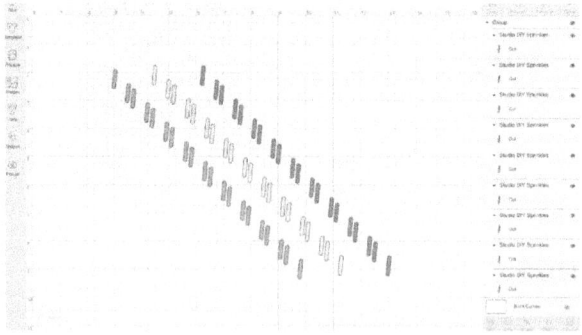

- This is how you can make a pattern for sprinkles for your iron-on. Make sure to size the elements to your preferred proportions and also prepare the design by clicking on "Mirror" – remember to use this command for designs that include iron-on vinyl. Once your design is ready, click on "Make it" and specify the material you are using – iron-on vinyl (Cricut iron-on).

- If you want to make a design for the entire front part of the shoe, you can create your pattern to fit the size of the shoes you are using, instead of applying vinyl in bits:

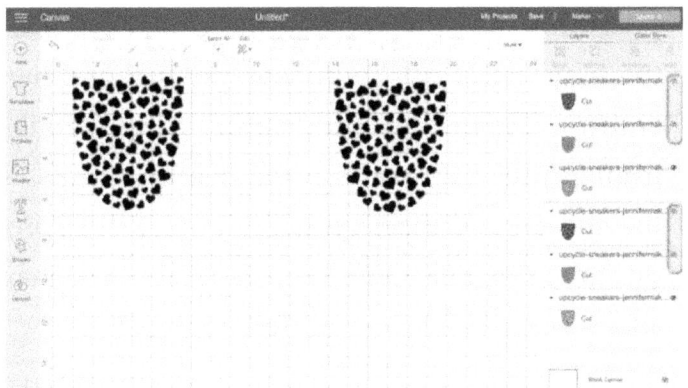

- Load your Cricut machine with vinyl – to fixate the vinyl, you can use tape to attach the edges of vinyl to the cutting mat. Once your design is cut out, use the weeding tool to peel off the excess vinyl and bits of vinyl and so that you bare left with your design. Now that your design is ready, it is time for the third step.

- It's right about time to give your iron or Easy Press a go. Heat the press and set the temperature to medium. Place a sock inside of the shoe to make a support and protect your fingers – the press and iron can burn your fingers by heating the canvas of the shoe – the sock is both practical and serves the purpose of taking precautions against potential burns. Place the vinyl by bits, one at a time, or as you find suitable based on your design.

- Put the press/iron over the vinyl part and on the canvas while holding the support from inside the shoe. Make sure to avoid other parts of the shoe other than canvas, like the rubber edges for example. Press against the canvas and vinyl for 20 seconds with a press/iron. Do not remove the protective sheet from the vinyl parts until you have pressed and heated the entire design. Once you are done with ironing/pressing, you can remove the sheets. Keeping the sheets on the design while ironing will protect the design from heat and keep it intact. You have your shoes ready to be worn, gifted or for sale.

Glasswork and Glass Etching

- Customizing glassware with etching? "Do tell more!", right? Imagine all the possibilities you have with etching as a technique and with the Cricut machine as your first and most important helper. You can customize any type of glassware, which includes glass mugs and cups and other glassware such as glass bowls and similar. Here is everything you need from start to finish so you could begin with etching glassware masterpieces.

Materials:

- Vinyl
- Stencil
- Transfer tape
- Glassware of your choice
- Etching cream
- Spatula
- Weeding tool
- Painting brush

Instructions:

- Upload SVG file with shapes and silhouettes you want to use for your glassware or find some designs you like in the library of images you have in the Design Space. You will need to resize or size the pieces to fit the size of your glassware and the part of the glassware you want to apply the vinyl to. Once the shapes are done and sized, you will need to set the line type to cut and choose vinyl as your material of choice after clicking on "Make it". Load the machine and fixate the vinyl piece before cutting.

- Once the design is cut out and ready, you will need to weed excess parts with the weeding tool. Weed out the positive part of your design – the inside of the design, so you are left with a pattern and substantial amount of vinyl around the shape. Next, you will apply the transfer tape on the piece of vinyl with the design pattern. Apply the tape with the vinyl on the glassware and smooth it out across the surface. Remove the transfer tape from the glassware.

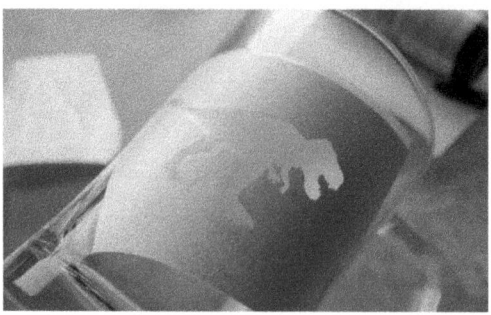

- Use the etching gel by applying it over the cutout part of the design and don't be afraid to use more etching glue as you want it to stick there. You will remove the excess gel later with a spatula. Before removing extra gel, you need to let the etching gel to sit for at least 20 minutes. Once the gel has settled, use the spatula to remove most of the gel.

- You don't need to throw your gel as you can reuse it – return it to the container and it will be good to use on more projects. After removing extra gel, remove the remaining gel by washing it with soap and warm water. Peel off the vinyl then give it another go with soap and warm water. Let the glassware dry and you have a masterpiece ready to be displayed and used.

Marbled Journal and Vinyl Art

Materials:

- Gold foil vinyl
- Marble paint – several colors of your choice
- White paint
- Transfer paint
- Disposable foil pan – to fit the notebook
- Kraft paper notebook
- Weeding tool
- Cricut machine

Instructions:

- For the first step you will leave the Design Space waiting as you are going to prepare the notebook and complete marbling first. Combining multiple crafting techniques is essential to becoming an advanced crafter, which is how you will make great use of this project. In case the cover of the notebook you are going to use for the project has a logo or images on it, use a layer of white paint to cover it up before marbling the cover with paint.

- Let the layer of white paint dry for a while as you are preparing the foil pan and marble paint. Fill up the foil pan with water then add the colors – only a drip or two of each color would be enough. Pour the paint drips in the center of the foil pan filled with water. Prepare the paper towels and sink the cover of the notebook into the foil pain. Hold it for a couple of seconds until the cover gets all the colors on, then place the paper towel between the cover and paper to prevent the water drops from reaching the paper inside the notebook.
- Let the marble paint on the cover dry as you are starting the Design Space and preparing vinyl for cutting.

Start a new project in the Design Space and upload the SVG file for letters and patterns you want to use on your notebook cover. You can also create your own design by using shapes, images, and letters available in the Design Space. Change the line type to cut once your design is ready. Set vinyl as your material of choice after you click on "Make it". Send the design to cutting after loading your machine with gold foil vinyl.

Use the weeding tool for removing the negative part of the vinyl design – the background. Peel off the bigger parts of the vinyl and scrape the rest with the help of your weeding tool. Apply the transfer tape on the vinyl design - make sure to size the transfer tape to fit the vinyl design. Apply the transfer tape with vinyl on the cover of the notebook. Smooth out the tape to remove any bubbles then remove the tape. You have just made your personal planner or an amazing gift for someone.

Customized Coffee Cups

Materials:

- Adhesive vinyl – permanent
- Cups – any type would work; you can buy reusable cups in bulks and get some in the size of Starbucks cups.
- Transfer tape
- Weeding tool
- Cricut machine

Instructions:

- Find and download, then upload SVG files for Starbucks-style cups or make your own to fit the Starbucks aesthetic.

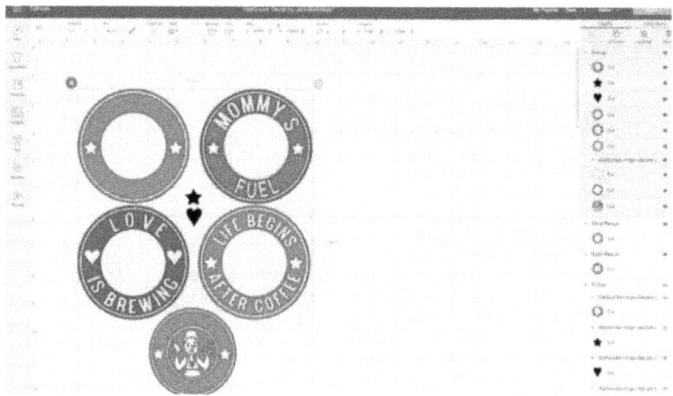

- You can also make your own by using shapes and designing tools in the Design Space. Make sure to measure the cups so that the personalized logo you are making is proportional to the size of the cup you are planning to customize. You can use shapes and letters with editing tools to make your own designs. Letters can be rotated to fit the shape of the circle design and you can use any font you like, write names or funny and witty statements. Make sure to set the line type for designs to "Cut". Once you are ready with editing and/or designing, you can click on "Make it" to proceed to cut. Specify vinyl as your material of choice when adjusting settings for cutting.

- It's time for weeding. Take your weeding tool and remove the parts of vinyl that you don't need in your design. Attach the transfer tape to the vinyl, and size the transfer tape to fit the size of the design you will use on the cup. Apply the vinyl with transfer tape on the cup and smooth the tape out to remove the bubbles. You can use a spatula for that, but your fingers would also do the work. Remove the transfer tape and your customized cup is good to go!

PROJECTS FOR INTERMEDIATE

Fabric Headband

Materials

- "Cricut Maker" or "Cricut Explore"
- Fabric grip mat, gray polka dot fabric, and thread, black or decorative elastic, home sewing machine.

Instructions

- Log into the "Design Space" application and click on the "New Project" button on the top right corner of the screen to view a blank canvas.
- Click on the "Projects" icon and type in "fabric headband" in the search bar.
- Click on "Customize" to further edit the project to your preference or simply click on the "Make It" button and load the fabric to your "Cricut" machine by placing the right side down on the mat and follow the instructions on the screen to cut your project.

- For assembly, measure your head where you would wear the headband and minus 15 inches from the measurement then cut the elastic at that length to use underneath the headband.
- Place the right sides together and pin the elastic inside with the ends sticking out that can be pinned at the end of the headband.
- Use the sewing machine sew around the outside edge of the headband, leaving 0.5-inch seam. Then sew over the ends of the elastic while it is between the two headband pieces leaving 2 inches opening unsewn along one side of the headband.
- Clip around the seam allowances with snips and turn the headband right side out. Use the end of a spoon to turn the edges of the headband out, then use an iron to press and solidify the shape.
- Top stich around the edge of the headband with a quarter-inch seam allowance for a finished look and close the turning hole.

Forever Fabric Banner

Materials

- "Cricut Maker" or "Cricut Explore"
- fabric grip mat
- glitter iron-on (black, pink)
- "Cricut Easy Press," weeded
- pink ribbon, canvas fabric
- sew able fabric stabilizer
- sewing machine and thread

Instructions

- Log into the "Design Space" application and click on the "New Project" button on the top right corner of the screen to view a blank canvas.
- Click on the "Projects" icon and type in "fabric banner" in the search bar.
- Click on "Customize" to further edit the project to your preference or simply click on the "Make It" button. Place the trimmed fabric on the cutting mat removing the paper backing, then load it to your "Cricut" machine and follow the instructions on the screen to cut your project. Similarly, load the iron-on vinyl sheet to the "Cricut" and cut the design, making sure to mirror the image.
- Carefully remove the excess material from the sheet using the "weeder tool," making sure only the design remains on the clear liner.
- Using the "Cricut EasyPress Mini" and "EasyPress Mat" the iron-on layers can be easily transferred to the fabric. Preheat your "EasyPress Mini" and put your iron-on vinyl design on the fabric and apply pressure for a

couple of minutes or more. Wait for a few minutes prior to peeling off the design while it is still warm.

Fabric Flower Brooch

Materials

- "Cricut Maker" or "Cricut Explore"
- fabric grip mat
- printable iron-on
- "Cricut EasyPress"
- Weeder
- fabric pencil pouch
- Inkjet printer

Instructions

- Log into the "Design Space" application and click on the "New Project" button on the top right corner of the screen to view a blank canvas.
- Click on the "Projects" icon and type in "fabric pouch" in the search bar.

31

- Click on "Customize" to further edit the project to your preference or simply click on the "Make It" button and follow the prompts on the screen for using ink jet printer to print the design on your printable vinyl and subsequently cut the design.
- Carefully remove the excess material from the sheet using the "weeder tool," making sure only the design remains on the clear liner.
- Using the "Cricut EasyPress Mini" and "EasyPress Mat" the iron-on layers can be easily transferred to the fabric. Preheat your "EasyPress Mini" and put your iron-on vinyl design on the fabric and apply pressure for a couple of minutes or more. Wait for a few minutes prior to peeling off the design while it is still warm.

Leather Flower Hat

Materials

- "Cricut Maker" or "Cricut Explore,"
- standard grip mat
- Cricut Faux Leather
- button, strong adhesive
- hat

Instructions

- Log into the "Design Space" application and click on the "New Project" button on the top right corner of the screen to view a blank canvas.
- Click on the "Projects" icon and type in "leather flower hat" in the search bar.
- Click on "Customize" to further edit the project to your preference or simply click on the "Make It" button and load the faux leather to your "Cricut" machine by placing it face down on the mat and follow the instructions on the screen to cut your project.
- For assembly, glue tabs on each flower together to give shape to every single layer and let dry.
- Glue all the flower layers on top of one another with the biggest layer at the bottom. Once the flower dries completely, glue button on the center of the flower. And finally, glue the flower to the hat.

Floral Mousepad

Materials

- "Cricut Maker" or "Cricut Explore"
- fabric grip mat

- printable fabric
- mousepad
- adhesive

Instructions

- Log into the "Design Space" application and click on the "New Project" button on the top right corner of the screen to view a blank canvas.
- Click on the "Images" icon on the "Design Panel" and type in "#MB145E" in the search bar. Select the image and click on the "Insert Images" button at the bottom of the screen.
- Edit the project to your preference or simply click on the "Make It" button and load the vinyl sheet to your "Cricut" machine and follow the instructions on the screen to print and cut your project.
- Once you have the printed fabric cut, use the adhesive to adhere it to the mousepad.

Jelly Bean Burp Cloth

Materials

- "Cricut Maker" or "Cricut Explore"
- fabric grip mat, fabric (light gray, teal)

- rotary cutter
- turning tool
- sewing machine
- thread

Instructions

- Log into the "Design Space" application and click on the "New Project" button on the top right corner of the screen to view a blank canvas.
- Click on the "Projects" icon and type in "jelly bean burp cloth" in the search bar.
- Click on "Customize" to further edit the project to your preference or simply click on the "Make It" button. Place the trimmed fabric on the cutting mat then load it to your "Cricut" machine and follow the instructions on the screen to cut your project. (Pay attention to the direction of the print for each fabric piece).
- Clip all curves generously and use a chopstick to turn the fabric pieces' right side out through the turning hole. Press all seams.
- Lastly, top stitch the entire shape and close the turning hole as well.

Personalized Coaster Tiles

Materials

- "Cricut Maker" or "Cricut Explore"
- standard grip mat
- "Cricut" iron-on lite
- freezer paper
- "Cricut EasyPress Mini"
- "EasyPress" mat
- weeding tool
- pillow cover
- screen print paint
- paintbrush

Instructions

- Log into the "Design Space" application and click on the "New Project" button on the top right corner of the screen to view a blank canvas.
- Click on the "Images" icon on the "Design Panel" and type in "#MED91E0" in the search bar. Select the image and click on the "Insert Images" button at the bottom of the screen.
- Edit the project to your preference or simply click on the "Make It" button and load the freezer paper with the non-shiny side up on the mat to your "Cricut" machine and follow the instructions on the screen to cut your project.

- Using a weeded tool, remove the negative space pieces of the design. Carefully place the stenciled quote on the pillow.
- Using the "Cricut EasyPress Mini" and "EasyPress Mat", iron on the design to the pillow. Preheat your "EasyPress Mini" and put your design on the desired area and apply pressure for couple of minutes or more. Remove the freezer paper and let it dry overnight.
- Set the paint with the "EasyPress" once again and enjoy your new pillow!

DIY PROJECTS

DIY Monogram Can Koozies

Instructions:

1. Measure your koozie tallness and width laying level and choose a fitting size (I picked mine to be 2.5" x 2.5").
2. In your plan space draw a circle that is the size you need your monogram to be (2.5"x 2.5").
3. Add a content box and your instructor's (or whomever you are making the koozie for) initials.
4. Decide on a text style (I utilized Effect).
5. Fit the initials to about the span of the circle.
6. Reduce letters until the point when each of the three letters are relatively contacting.

7. Ungroup letters and stretch center letters to be as tall as the most astounding point on a circle (additionally influence center introductory slenderer if should be).
8. Stretch outside letters to be around 75% stature of the center beginning (you will most likely need to thin these letters out as well).
9. Using your Cricut to remove the monogram of Iron on Vinyl (make a point to identical representation so it prints in reverse).
10. Iron on to koozie (for full instructional exercise on the best way to apply press on vinyl see this post).

Add your educators' most loved pop to koozie and a couple of additional for them to appreciate as well.

Oogie Boogie Treat Packs

Make these Bad dreams Before Christmas enlivened cute gift packs in under 15 minutes with your Cricut.

Supplies:

- Burlap Support Packs
- Black Warmth Exchange (Press On) Vinyl
- Treats/Treats
- Cricut Producer or Investigate Air
- Heat Press or Iron

Directions:

1. Open Oogie Boogie record in Configuration Space (this is an awesome instructional exercise that demonstrates to well-ordered industry standards to transfer pictures in configuration space).
2. Change the extent of your Okogie Boogie face to accommodate your packs (I made mine 2" tall).
3. Duplicate outlines until the point when you have the same number of appearances as you do packs.
4. Load warmth exchange vinyl gleaming side down on light grasp slicing mat and send to cut.
5. Weed overabundance vinyl from around appearances and separate faces (the fundamental toolbox proves to be useful with this).
6. Preheat burlap sacks before squeezing (either with an iron or warmth press for no less than 5 seconds).
7. I found through experimentation that you have to push down longer on burlap to get the vinyl to stick. I've discovered that squeezing at 275° for 45 seconds gets everything squeezed splendidly.
8. Slowly peel plastic support from the left corner.
9. Fill your treat packs with fun treats.

Teacher Tumbler Blessing Thought

For this venture you will require:

- Images from Configuration Space
- black, red, green and dark colored vinyl light grasp cutting mat
- transfer tape
- tumblers

Directions:

1. First, you'll open up your plan. TIP: I gauged my glass and knew I had around a 3 in x 4 spot to work with. So, I made a square shape that is the correct shape in Configuration Space.
2. Then I estimated these charming instructor statements to fit perfectly! :)
3. I erased the square shape, and now it's an ideal opportunity to cut!

4. I sent everything to my Cricut Investigate Air 2 to do the hard stuff! Cutting! :)
5. Vinyl arrives in a strong sheet with a sponsorship paper. Your machine really cuts the vinyl, not the support paper. It is anything but a printer, it's a shaper. ;)
6. The following stage is called weeding. Fundamentally you are expelling all the abundance vinyl from around your plan.
7. Then you'll put a bit of exchange over your vinyl.
8. Now, we are prepared to apply the vinyl.
9. Remove the sponsorship paper, leaving the vinyl on the exchange tape. When you are working with a bended surface work on the center and then out. Rub the center of your decal onto your surface, and after that delicately rub the vinyl down toward the two edges.
10. Then deliberately expel the exchange tape, abandoning the vinyl.
11. The apple is simply layered red, green, dark colored and dark vinyl.
12. Then I filled the tumblers with hot chocolate parcels and chocolates.

Diy Magnet Chore Chart

Materials:

- Cookie Sheet (I utilized this two pack – idealize estimate!)
- Clear glass marbles with level edge – 1"
- Adhesive Magnet Paper (simply ensure it's sufficiently thin to be cut by your machine.
- Printable Sticker Paper
- Deep Cut cutting edge
- Adhesive Vinyl or Cement Thwart in shade of decision
- Transfer Tape
- Design Space Task for Magnets and Vinyl

Guidelines:

1. Open up the Outline Space Task and select to tweak it. You can change the name, text style utilized, and so on in this document before we begin (or include diverse errands).
2. Follow these guidelines for how to make magnets with Cricut. You can skirt the part about making them and go straight to stage four. In the event that you need to include new errands that I did exclude, you can take after the initial steps to perceive how I did that.
3. Once the materials have been removed, get rid of the overabundance material
4. and, utilizing exchange tape, exchange the material to your treat plate.
5. And presently, you're finished!

Diy Grinch Glasses

These Grinch glasses are anything but difficult to make and ideal for your vacation get together.

To influence the glasses, you'll need to begin by painting the stems of the containers with the green paint. You don't have to have it too thick in light of the fact that the sparkle will help cover the glass.

Sprinkle the sparkle on top of it. It's most effortless on the off chance that you do this over a paper towel that way you can simply get the towel when you're set and pour the abundance sparkle back in the jug.

you'll need to remove the Grinch face of vinyl.

Use exchange tape to join the vinyl to the highest point of the glass.

Furthermore, there you have it. I made 8 of these glasses in under 30 minutes (you'll need to give the sparkle and paint a chance to set up for a couple of hours before serving however). The best part is they were plastic so I didn't need to stress over them breaking when and on the off chance that they get dropped.

GIFT IDEAS

Making a Baby Elephant for a Birthday Gift

DIY baby presents are so enjoyable to create for the receiver and signify very much. Customized baby products for newborns are so good, wouldn't you say? Customized gifts of your living might not get any cuter than one for a newborn child.

They also don't have to be complicated. You can build this birth stat elephant for every kid to enjoy and parents to swoon about with a Cricut cutting tool and some HTV.

The supplies:

- (Elephant) plush doll
- Simple Mat for Pressing
- Cutting Unit for Cricuts
- The Quick Press 2
- Vinyl iron-on
- Mat and Equipment Cricut

Directions:-How to:

1. In Cricut Software, you could conveniently model your birth statistics yourself but click here if you have Cricut and want to use this prototype.
2. In reality, I traced the elephant's ear and submitted it to the CDS so that I could weigh it. I ended up having the

monogram's name between 2.3 "x2.3" and the birth numbers 2.5 "around 3.5" strong.
3. Take out the HTV photos. Be sure to switch on the reflection setting on the preview screen and put the HTV with the shiny side down on your pad. On an iron-on framework, cut it.
4. I did not connect all of my own because I needed to be able to position them manually.
5. Weed off the excess vinyl and remove the acrylic backing such that the birth stats have different parts.
6. Adjust the timer on the tiny Easy Press to 315F because the elephant is a polymer. If you need further assistance on how to use Easy Press, be sure to check out my analysis of Cricut Easy Press 2.
7. This will also be the great Easy Press Mini project (I already didn't have one when I created this elephant souvenir of birth status!)
8. Push the ears for several moments to bring the humidity out after the Easy Press has been preheated (it just takes a few seconds). Add the biggest text parts to the ear where you like them to be.
9. Although I'm going to click twice (kind of like stacking), I'm going to click them on that little bit separately.
10. On the Simple Button, button the first surface with two hands and a ton of body mass for about 5 seconds. To chill the iron-on, wait 35 seconds and then take off the backrest.
11. Place the other birth stats where you like them and ensure sure they don't clash with the acrylic backings.

Place the whole ear off a Teflon or waterproof layer and push gently for 25-30 seconds.
12. Have the rubber backing off. Turn the elephant over and click for 15 seconds
13. on the back of the hand. In reality, pushing the rear allows the HTV to stick even further.
14. Repeat with the other ear the same measures. Pressure the word logo for several moments then focuses it.
15. Push for 3-5 seconds with two hands and with a lot of body strength. Let 30 of them cool down and then strip the polyurethane coating—the Word Core.
16. For 30-35 seconds, protect with a safe sheet and click. Break the rubber, turn over the elephant, and push for 20 seconds on the other side. If you have a Cricut Manufacturer, it will go fine with an etched birth status plaque.

Customized Suede Diary

Create a DIY suede diary with a good statement from Dr. Martin Luther King, Jr.

The engraving went well, but I still wanted to make the quote stick out, so I ended up using pens for the Draw element. Below, I will show you both directions!

Supplies:

- I used silver cloth-Cricut cloth.
- Cutting blade of intense slashing for housing

- Cricut maker,
- Alternative-Cricut pens
- Cardstock
- Good pad for grip and normal pad
- Twine, ribbon, or thick loop
- Cricut DIY Suede Diary

Directions for the Cricut Suede Book:

1. In Cricut Control, I found a Suede diary project that was comparable to just what I tried to create but modified some of it. It was named the "Notebook for Suggestions." This is what I love about the Personalize feature!
2. This project can be located at Cricut Software by clicking here.
3. Snapshot screen
4. I opened it up and expanded all the bits, and modified the writing on the notebook afterward. I detached the current text and then put the quotation I needed into the text box.
5. I chose Engrave from the Line type menu since I intended to get the quotation embossed in the suede. I picked both the text and Diary cover and pressed Click until I had the font I needed and the layout I needed it to be.
6. Suede CDs from Engrave Suede
7. I chose shiny suede from the settings menu and put my suede, bright side up, on a solid grip pad. Usually, with the shiny side down, you can cut cloth, but I wanted the right side up because I was engraving it.

8. When cutting dense stuff, ensure the white skids are placed to the sides. CDS guided me first to attach the engraving edge. Making sure you follow the top or side of the video to see all this in full detail!
9. To try to make the engraving deeper, I run it through one more time, and then I placed the deeper point blade when asked to cut the edges. This is how the engraved suede felt.

Cutting Cricut Suede

I like it, but I believe I still want stuff to always stick out because of my old eyes because I can understand them! So, I went back in and, after detaching the email, I modified Engrave to Sketch. I re-attached the text to the cover after adjusting it to print.

Cricut drawing on suede

You may either use Cricut Explore Air or Cricut Creator from this point on. I might have done both designing and slicing suede with a Cricut Explore Air if I hadn't tried to emboss it with a Cricut Builder blade.

Then, in clamp B, I filled the pen and placed the pad again. The text is slightly off at the engraved script because I had to reload the pad, but I sort of liked the result!

I unloaded the pad when it was finished, and then laid out the remaining white

cardstock Diary pages on a normal grip pad. A couple of pads were used to cut all the sheets.

Sketch and cut on suede

I cut the surplus Suede and then flipped over my pad to peel the Suede sheet off. I stripped them all off the pads, the same thing I did for the cardstock bits.

Placing together the DIY suede Notebook

It's time to organize the Diary until all the bits are removed. Let the ink dry on the suede to prevent it from smearing! You might even type with a small Sharpie, too.

There is one major piece of cardstock. It sits on the back of the sheet. And, like a slice, all the papers go in between.

Mark both of the gaps out. One is at the peak and one on the floor. Using a

ribbon, twine, a heavy cord, whatever you want the notebook to keep together. Push it through the suede's bottom hole and all the pages, bring it across the back, and finally stick it thru the top hole.

All ends are going to be on the front side. Don't lock it too far, so when you remove it, you're not going to be able to put it flatly. Then attach or make a front angle bow, and you're done!

Mr. and Mrs. Gift Mugs

Detail of Materials:

- Tape Move
- Device for Scraper
- Mat Cutting
- Yellow Chrome Vinyl Adhesive
- Plain Mugs
- Cricut maker or an equivalent device
- Device for Weeding

Directions:

1. Phase One: Upload Concepts and Set-Up
2. Start downloading from Mrs. and Mr. SVG and download them to Cricut software. Evaluate and then adjust the patterns to match the cup you're creating. You may either drag the cursor in the corners OR directly insert the measurements in the scale window.
3. Press Progress, and then in the cut settings pane, pick Metallic Vinyl.
4. Stage Two: Vinyl Fill and Cut
5. To commence cutting, click the blinking start icon. Chrome vinyl slices more easily than I've dealt on any other vinyl.
6. Stage Three: Weeding the Design
7. Cut the photographs away from the vinyl board, then pick the discarded bits using a weeding tool.
8. Phase Four: Transfer Decals
9. Cut a sheet of transfer tape over the adhesive vinyl and stick it. With a separator instrument or anything similar, sweep well over it.

10. Center on the mug with the decal and apply strong pressure. I prefer to just use my fingertips on curved surfaces like this, but the scraper tool may be used as well.
11. Peel the transfer tape clear, leaving only the decal on the cup unchanged.
12. To build the matching package, repeat the steps above!
13. For lasting installations such as bottles and drinking glasses, gloss sticky adhesive is suitable. To increase the vinyl's effectiveness, please make sure to advise the receivers to hand wash their mugs.

Christmas Sweet Jar

It's still enjoyable to offer presents, so it makes things all that much cooler when you take a personalized present, place it in a container, and send it to a friend. Today, I'm showing you how simple it is to use adhesive vinyl to transform a simple glass bottle into a nice Christmas Eve gift package. Let's share the joy for Christmas, y' all!

Required Supplies:

- Scraper The Scraper
- Tape Move
- Vinyl Glue
- Device for Weeding
- Similar Gifts
- Container of Glass
- Mat Cutting

Directions: -

1. Phase One: The Set-Up Template
2. Work in Cricut Software, but in Silhouette Studio, you could also do this. Download the template and change the colors to fit the vinyl shades you are going to use.
3. Select the "Create It" button, and you will be directed by the program through the steps of charging and slicing each individual vinyl paint. Note, sticky vinyl with the colored side faced up, and the plain sheet covering facing up on the sheet is put on the cutting mat.
4. Stage Two: Prototypes for Cut and weeding
5. Strip the unwanted design from across the models after the slicing is complete, then weeding out the smaller pieces.
6. Phase Three: Switch Tape Attach
7. To add firm pressure, cut the tape's top to match over the template and use the scraper method.
8. Phase Four: Transferring Designs to Container
9. To burnish well on the logo, line the open spaces on the container and use the scraper method again. When you

operate on a curved surface, beginning from the middle and working your way back, it is simpler to implement the pattern.
10. Remove the transfer film, leaving only the vinyl decal behind.
11. To implement the second part of the template, repeat the steps above.
12. The container looks so festive and cute and couldn't have been simpler to do.
13. Optional: Making Customized Items
14. So, I figured it would be extra nice to design the cups to mean something nice. My neighbor has two small children.
15. Fill and Supply with Presents!
16. With some new cheesecakes, sweets colored wrappers, cotton candy, mini gummy bears, Christmas shaped towels, and those cool design tent key rings, I filled up this nice little container.
17. With a festive bow, tie it all together and leave it on the door for a nice surprise!

PROJECTS IDEAS WITH GLASS

Etched Monogrammed Glass

Etched Monogrammed Glass Glasses are one of the most-used things in your kitchen, and it's impossible to have too many of them. It's actually quite easy to customize them with etching, and it will look as if a professional did it. Simply use glass etching cream that you can find at any craft store! Be sure to read the instructions and warning labels carefully before you begin. The vinyl will act as a stencil, protecting the parts of the glass that you don't want to etch. Be sure to take your time to get the vinyl smooth against the glass, especially where there are small bits. You don't want any of the cream to get under the edge of the vinyl. You can use the Cricut Explore One, Cricut Explore Air 2, or Cricut Maker for this project.

Supplies Needed

- A glass of your choice – make sure that the spot you want to monogram is smooth

- Vinyl
- Cutting mat
- Weeding tool or pick
- Glass etching cream

Instructions

1. Open Cricut Design Space and create a new project.
2. Select the "Image" button in the Design Panel and search for "monogram."
3. Choose your favorite monogram and click "Insert."
4. Place your vinyl on the cutting mat.
5. Send the design to your Cricut.
6. Use a weeding tool or pick to remove the monogram, leaving the vinyl around it.
7. Remove the vinyl from the mat.
8. Carefully apply the vinyl around your glass, making it as smooth as possible, particularly around the monogram.
9. If you have any letters with holes in your monogram, carefully reposition those cutouts in their proper place.
10. Following the instructions on the etching cream, apply it to your monogram.
11. Remove the cream and then the vinyl.
12. Give your glass a good wash.

Live, Love, Laugh Glass Block

Glass blocks are an inexpensive yet surprisingly versatile craft material. You can find them at both craft and hardware stores. They typically have a hole with a lid so that you can fill the blocks with the items of your choice. This project uses tiny fairy lights for a glowing quote block, but you can fill it however you'd like. The frost spray paint adds a bit of elegance to the glass and diffuses the light for a softer glow, hiding the string of the fairy lights.

Holographic vinyl will add to the magical look, but you can use whatever colors you'd like. This features a classic quote that's great to have around your house, but you can change it. You can use the Cricut Explore One, Cricut Explore Air 2, or Cricut Maker for this project.

Supplies Needed

- Glass block
- Frost spray paint
- Clear enamel spray
- Holographic vinyl
- Vinyl transfer tape
- Cutting mat
- Weeding tool or pick
- Fairy lights

Instructions

1. Spray the entire glass block with frost spray paint, and let it dry.
2. Spray the glass block with a coat of clear enamel spray, and let it dry.
3. Open Cricut Design Space and create a new project.
4. Select the "Text" button in the Design Panel.
5. Type "Live Love Laugh" in the text box.
6. Use the dropdown box to select your favorite font.
7. Arrange the words to sit on top of each other.
8. Place your vinyl on the cutting mat.
9. Send the design to your Cricut.
10. Use a weeding tool or pick to remove the excess vinyl from the design.
11. Apply transfer tape to the design.
12. Remove the paper backing and apply the words to the glass block.
13. Smooth down the design and carefully remove the transfer tape.
14. Place fairy lights in the opening of the block, leaving the battery pack on the outside.

Unicorn Wine Glass

Who doesn't love unicorns? Who doesn't love wine? Bring them together with these glittery wine glasses! The outdoor vinyl will hold up to use and washing, and the Mod Podge will keep the glitter in place for years to come.

Customize it even more with your own quote. You could use a different magical creature as well—mermaids go great with glitter too! Customize this to suit your tastes or to create gifts for your friends and family.

Consider using these for a party and letting the guests take them home as favors! You can use the Cricut Explore One, Cricut Explore Air 2, or Cricut Maker for this project.

Supplies Needed

- Stemless wine glasses
- Outdoor vinyl in the color of your choice
- Vinyl transfer tape
- Cutting mat
- Weeding tool or pick
- Extra fine glitter in the color of your choice Mod Podge

Instructions

1. Open Cricut Design Space and create a new project.
2. Select the "Text" button in the Design Panel.
3. Type "It's not drinking alone if my unicorn is here."
4. Using the dropdown box, select your favorite font.
5. Adjust the positioning of the letters, rotating some to give a whimsical look.
6. Select the "Image" button on the Design Panel and search for "unicorn."

7. Select your favorite unicorn and click "Insert," then arrange your design how you want it on the glass.
8. Place your vinyl on the cutting mat, making sure it is smooth and making full contact.
9. Send the design to your Cricut.
10. Use a weeding tool or pick to remove the excess vinyl from the design. Use the Cricut BrightPad to help if you have one.
11. Apply transfer tape to the design, pressing firmly and making sure there are no bubbles.
12. Remove the paper backing and apply the words to the glass where you'd like them. Leave at least a couple of inches at the bottom for the glitter.
13. Smooth down the design and carefully remove the transfer tape.
14. Coat the bottom of the glass in Mod Podge, wherever you would like glitter to be. Give the area a wavy edge.
15. Sprinkle glitter over the Mod Podge, working quickly before it dries.
16. Add another layer of Mod Podge and glitter, and set it aside to dry.
17. Cover the glitter in a thick coat of Mod Podge.
18. Allow the glass to cure for at least 48 hours.

PROJECT IDEAS AT HOME

Flower Garden Tote Bag

Supplies:

- Canvas tote bag
- White heat transfer vinyl
- Cricut Easy Press or iron
- Cutting mat
- Weeding tool or pick

Instructions:

1. Open Cricut Design Space and create a new project.
2. Select the "Image" button in the lower left-hand corner and search "flowers."
3. Choose your favorite flower and click "Insert."
4. Continue with a variety of flowers, lining them up together to form a straight edge at the bottom.
5. Place your vinyl on the cutting mat.
6. Send the design to your Cricut.

7. Use a weeding tool or pick to remove the excess vinyl from the design.
8. Place the design along the bottom of the tote bag with the plastic side up.
9. Carefully iron on the design.
10. After cooling, peel away the plastic by rolling it.
11. Carry around your new garden tote bag!

Wild OX Plaid No-Sew Reindeer Cushion

Supplies:

- Buffalo Plaid Texture
- Pillow Cover
- Pillow Embed
- Heat'n'Bond Ultra Hold
- Cricut Creator
- 12"x24" Pink Cutting Mat (in case you're utilizing a littler pad you can utilize a 12"x12" pink tangle)
- Cricut EasyPress

Instructions

1. Open up Configuration Space and alter the measure of your reindeer if necessary. My cushion was 20"x20" so

my reindeer is around 9"x14". TIP: when attempting to choose how enormous to influence a picture, to go into Formats and pick from more than 100 unique choices including pads, shirts, entryways, windows, flip failures and that's just the beginning!
2. Measure a couple of inches additional and cut a bit of Heat'n'Bond. Append to the back of your texture with the paper side far from your texture. Attach the texture with Heat'n'Bond to your pink cutting mat texture side up.
3. Send tasks to be cut. **Make beyond any doubt you have your rotating cutting edge in the B clasp on your Maker*
4. Preheat your cushion case with your EasyPress for around 510 seconds.
5. Place your reindeer on your pillowcase and utilize a ruler to quantify focus.
6. Apply EasyPress with a medium weight to your reindeer and apply (300° for 30 seconds). On the off chance that your reindeer is bigger than 9"x9", you'll need to do this progression twice, once for the best, once for the base. **Make beyond any doubt you are doing this on a solid surface, similar to kitchen countertops**
7. Flip pillowcase over and rehash past advance.
8. Embed cushion and appreciate it!

Framed Succulents Made from Paper

Supplies:

- Foam brush
- Standard grip cutting mat
- DecoArt acrylic paint for the frame
- Scissors to curl the succulent petals
- A piece of chipboard, cardstock, or cardboard
- 12x12 cardstock in assorted green colors
- Glue gun

Instructions:

1. Start with painting the picture frame that you wish to use. Unless you wish to leave it rustic and old as I would.
2. Place your chipboard or cardboard to the inside of the frame. This is for placing the succulents on. Use the hot glue gun to place it in the frame properly.
3. Next, find the image of the file that you wish to use. Press Go to cut out the succulents.

4. Once all the pieces have been cut from the paper then you can begin to assemble the pieces to make your succulent.
5. Once the succulents are created, you can begin to glue them to a board.

Wooden Hand Lettered Sign

Supplies:

- Acrylic paint for whatever colors you would like
- Vinyl
- Cricut Explore Air 2
- Walnut hollow basswood planks
- Transfer Tape
- Scraper
- An SVG file or font that you wish to use
- Pencil
- Eraser

Instructions

1. You will need to start by deciding what you will want to draw onto the wood.
2. Then, place some lines on the plank to designate the horizontal and vertical axis for the grid. Set this aside for later.
3. Upload the file that you wish to use to the Design Space. Then, cut the file with the proper setting for vinyl.
4. Weed out the writing or design spaces that are not meant to go on the wood.
5. Using the transfer tape, apply the tape to the top of the vinyl and smooth it out. Using the scraper and the corner of the transfer paper, slowly peel the backing off a bit at a time. Do it carefully.
6. Remove the backing of the vinyl pieces, aligning the lettering or design so that it is fully centered. Place it carefully on the wooden plank.
7. Again, use the scraper to smooth out the vinyl on the plank.
8. Take off the transfer tape by smoothing off the bubbles as you scrape along the wood sign. Discard the transfer tape at that time.
9. Continue to use the scraper to make the vinyl smoother. There should be no bumps since this creates bleeding.
10. Now, paint your wood plank with any color of your choice. Peel the vinyl letters off. Once the paint has completely dried, you can erase your pencil marks.

Hexie Hand Towels

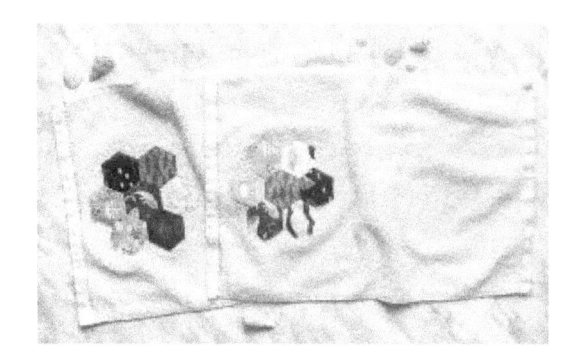

Supplies:

- Fabric
- Cardstock
- Needle
- Thread
- Embroidery Band
- Embroidery String
- Thermoweb Texture Breaker
- Craft Clasps
- Tea Towel

Instructions

1. The most effective method to Sew Hexies – English Paper Piecing Instructional exercise:
2. To start you will require a hexagon layout.
3. Place the hexagon over the texture and cut the texture around 1/2 bigger than the format on each of the 6 sides. For this task, you will need to particular cut the texture. That way to explicitly put the hexagon over a specific outline and after that cut around it.

4. If you have a Cricut Creator you can do this with the SnapMat to get consummately set hexies.
5. Fold the texture from one side of the hexagon over the layout as appeared in the photograph underneath and secure it with an Art Clasp. This will shield the texture from moving around while you are sewing it.
6. Finger press the crease, turn the hexagon, and overlay throughout the following side making a pleasant sharp point. Finger squeeze this crease also.
7. Thread a needle and bunch the end. Embed the needle just before the wrinkle, sew through the opposite sides to join them together. Ensure that the needle does not experience the format.
8. Repeat this procedure around the whole hexagon.
9. Each side will cover the opposite side. Keep the texture pulled rigid without misshaping it.
10. Once you've achieved the starting tie off the string.
11. With a hot iron, press the hexie.
12. Aren't these hexies simply lovable?
13. Once you have sewn each of the five hexies it's an ideal opportunity to join them together
14. Place the hexagons with the right sides together.
15. Insert the needle through the tip of the corner to anchor the hexies together and pull the string until the point when you achieve the bunch toward the end.
16. You will combine the hexies utilizing little whipstitches. Painstakingly whipstitch the whole edge together taking consideration not to sew into the format.

17. Repeat this procedure with each of the five hexagons ensuring they are arranged appropriately before sewing them together.
18. Once every one of the five hexies is combined lay them over the tea towel.
19. At this point, you can whipstitch the whole shape to the tea towel or utilize the Thermoweb Texture Circuit to connect them.
20. Once the hexies have been joined and have had adequate time to dry, put a weaving band over the towel and utilize weaving floss to complete a backstitch around the edge of the hexagon shape.
21. Presently it's a great opportunity to hang up your cute hexie drying towel and respect your diligent work!

DIY Baby Milestone Blanket

Supplies:

- Cricut Machine
- Cricut EasyPress or Iron

- 23 sheets press on
- 1 1/4-yard white bandage texture
- Cricut Configuration Space document
- Autumn in November textual style

Instructions

1. When utilizing Cricut Press On, it's imperative to make sure to reflect the picture. You'll put it glossy side down on the tangle and cut utilizing the iron-on setting. Try not to utilize the HTV setting with your Creator. For reasons unknown, it is slicing through. You simply need it to cut the vinyl and keep the transporter sheet unblemished.
2. You'll evacuate all the negative space and after that cut every month number with the goal that you can space them on your cover. When utilizing the Cricut EasyPress, you require a hard surface and afterward a collapsed towel on that hard surface. You require something that will give a little with the goal that every one of the edges will be safely followed. You know you've got an awesome grip when you can see the material's surface.
3. For Iron On Lite, you'll require a temperature of 305F and afterward press for 2530 seconds. Give your things a decent warm-up in advance and after you're finished squeezing, turn your material over and press again for a couple of more seconds.
4. Now you're finished. So super simple yet it requires a tad of investment to get your numbers equitably dispersed and to complete the edges of your material. You'll never need to spend $40+ on a Millstone infant cover again.

5. These DIY infant breakthrough covers are the best child shower blessings you can give. They're far superior knowing you put your diligent work into something so unique.

SOME MORE IDEAS

Pumpkin Pillows

Materials:

- Burlap pad spread
- Printable heat transfer
- Material paper (whenever required for your image)
- Iron
- Printer and ink
- Pumpkin record of your choice

Steps

1. Download the pumpkin records that you want to use to your PC as a jpg document. Utilize the transfer button in configuration space to import. For the blue pumpkin particularly, make certain to pick the unpredictable picture type. The other two imported fine with the reasonably unpredictable setting.

2. When you add to the canvas, you can see that it is a print. At that point cut by the layer's menu on the correct hand side. Resize to whatever size you require for your

pumpkin pad. You should remember the size of your heat transfer. The Cricut will likewise print an outskirt around the picture so as to see it on the machine. It will have to be adjusted if the picture is too huge to even consider fitting with the fringe.
3. Press start and wait until it ready and you can cut it. Ensure that the material size is right for your before you begin to heat transfer.

Burlaps

Materials:

- Burlap (a genuinely tight weave works best)
- Shabby Glue
- Pouncer brush
- Wax paper
- Cricut Maker
- Cricut Strong Grip move tape
- Cricut green tangle

- Earthenware pot (roughly 3 creeps in distance across at the top)
- Styrofoam ball
- Greenery
- Craft glue and paste firearm
- Cricut delicious document

Steps:

1. Start with a 12 x 12 square of burlap and lay it on to ensure your work surface. Blend the paste creamer in with water. At that point use a pouncer brush to apply this blend all over your burlap.
2. Allow it to dry. This might take a long time. At that point simply strip your hardened burlap from the wax paper sheet. Presently we need to get this solid material to adhere to a Cricut tangle. Apply solid grasp move tape to the rear of your burlap. At that point place the non-clingy side of your exchange tape down onto your tangle. Press it down truly well. You can even utilize a brayer or moving pin here.

Felt Banners

Materials:

- Dowel slice to 5.5"
- Felt
- Heated glue
- Yarn

Steps:

1. Plug in your heated glue firearm to get it warmed up, at that point cut your felt utilizing the turning sharp edge and texture tangle. Strip away the additional felt.
2. Strip off the flag. Spot the dowel on top, and crease over the top edge to see where the dowel should be set.
3. Include a line of craft glue.
4. Carefully overlay the top over. On the off chance that you have a low-temp stick firearm, or thick felt, you may have the option to squeeze it down with your fingers… yet to be protected you could utilize a pencil or the rest of the dowel so you don't burn your fingers.

Coffee Sleeves

Materials:

- Felt (I used the Cricut felt sheets)
- Iron on Vinyl (I used the sparkle vinyl in silver)
- Cricut Cutting Machine
- Weeding instruments (optional)
- Cricut Easy-Press (optional)
- Velcro
- Texture paste or sewing machine
- Cut document

Steps:

1. Start by cutting your pieces. Cut the words from sparkle iron on vinyl utilizing your fine point cutting edge. Make sure to reflect the cuts on the iron on vinyl and spot its glossy side down on your tangle. Cut the sleeve itself from felt. On the off chance that you need to mark your cutting two of the sleeves one after another, you might need to change the situation inside Design Space to capitalize on your material. It needs to cut every sleeve from one sheet of felt.
2. Start by featuring your first tangle with a sleeve. At that point click on the sleeve itself.
3. Next snap the second tangle that has a sleeve. Snap the sleeve itself and snap the three dabs. At that point pick "move to another tangle".
4. Pick the tangle with the principal sleeve.
5. Presently you simply need to turn it and move the position, so it isn't covering the first. You would now be able to cut two sleeves from one sheet of felt.

6. Remove all material from your vinyl pattern including the focuses of your letters.

3D Butterfly Wall Art

Materials

- Cricut holographic sparkle unicorn removable vinyl in pink, teal, and silver
- Cricut essentials removable vinyl in gold and wine
- Cricut glitter cardstock in wine, gold, silver, lavender, pink, and blue
- Cricut glitter tape in pink
- Green StandardGrip mat
- Cricut Fine-Point Blade
- Weeding tool
- Scraping tool or brayer tool
- Pair of scissors for cutting the material to size
- Glue dots or 2-way tape for sticking cardstock to the wall
- Tape measure
- Pencil
- Rubbing alcohol

Directions:

1. Open a new project in Design Space.
2. Select 'Images' from the menu on the left-hand side.
3. Choose a picture of a butterfly; this project uses #M28D239 as an example.
4. Unlock the butterfly and change the dimensions to 24" wide and 24" long.
5. This makes the butterfly 2' by 2.'
6. The butterfly wings will be in three different colors with the tail of each wing extending out with the glitter tape.
7. The smaller 3D butterflies will fly out from the glitter tape.
8. To slice the butterfly, you will need to use a technique called contouring.
9. Duplicate the butterfly and move the duplicated image off to one side out of the way.
10. Select the original butterfly image.
11. On the bottom right-hand menu where you find the Slice, Weld, Attach, and Flatten options, you will see the Contour option.
12. Select the 'Contour' option.
13. A box will appear on the screen with the butterfly image in the main pane and images in the right-hand panel.
14. You can zoom the butterfly to 50% in order to see what you are doing if it appears too large in the viewing frame.
15. To do this, you will find the zoom bar in the main panel at the bottom left-hand corner.
16. You are going to select various pieces of the butterfly's wing to hide, so you only have the body and bottom

wings leftover. It will all make sense once you have done it.

17. Using the images in the right-hand panel, select the shapes in the boxes in the right-hand panel that match up with the shapes in the top wings.
18. As you click on a shape in the right-hand panel, it will grey out in the viewing window.
19. If you accidentally select one of the bottom wings or the abdomen, simply click on the shape again and it will reappear.
20. Once you have finished greying out the top wings, select the 2 antennae as well.
21. You will also want to select the 2 long wing tailpieces at the bottom of the butterfly.
22. There are two small pieces that are in the middle of the abdomen and just above the bottom wings that you will want to keep.
23. Click the 'X' in the top right-hand corner of the 'Hide Contour' box.
24. The butterfly will now appear without the top wings, antennae, and wing tails on the grid.
25. Change the color to light blue and move the image to one side.
26. Move the duplicated full butterfly to the workspace.
27. Select the full butterfly and repeat steps 11 to 23. Get rid of the abdomen, bottom wings, and tail as well as those two little pieces halfway down the body.
28. Leave only the top wings and antennae.
29. When you are done contouring the top part of the butterfly, change the color to armadillo.

30. If you put your two shapes together, they will line up perfectly.
31. You will now be able to cut them in two different colors.
32. Save the project.
33. Use the silver holographic vinyl for the antennae and the top wings.
34. Use the teal holographic vinyl for the abdomen and bottom wings.
35. Measure the space on the wall, marking it off with the pencil.
36. Wipe down the surface with a clean cloth and the rubbing alcohol. You can use any product to clean the surface that has an instant dry and leaves no residue.
37. Once the images for the butterfly have been cut, use transfer tape cut to size to transfer the images onto the wall starting with the bottom wings and abdomen.
38. You are not going to want to have the vinyl transfer over the bottom part.
39. Before you apply the transfer tape to the top wings, cut around the bottom section where the abdomen will go. Leave a gap so that the vinyl does not layer over the bottom part.
40. Cut the transfer tape into the same shape, then transfer the wings onto the wall lining them up with the body and bottom wings.
41. Cut two ½" wide by 3" long glitter ribbon pieces and give them a swallowtail cut at the one end.
42. Cut off the inside part of the swallowtail, leaving the tape to taper off to a single point.

43. You may want to reinforce the tape's stickiness by giving it a few glue dots.
44. Apply 1 ribbon over each of the butterfly's tail wings, leaving only the top funnel bit leading from the wing in vinyl.
45. Open a new project in Design Space.
46. Select 'Images' from the menu on the left-hand side.
47. Choose the same picture of a butterfly—#M28D239.
48. Unlock the butterfly and change the dimensions to 3.15" wide and 2.33" long.
49. From the top menu, set the 'Linetype' to 'Cut.'
50. Leave the color as it is.
51. Save the project.
52. Click 'Make it'
53. You can fit 12 butterflies on a sheet of 12" by 12" cardstock.
54. You can make 72 butterflies with the 6 different glitter cardstock colors.
55. Set the 'Project copies' to 72 and click 'Apply.'
56. This selection will load 6 cutting boards with 12 butterflies per board.
57. Select each board and lay the butterflies out with enough room between, above, and below them.
58. Use the glitter cardstock and load a different color card each time you are ready to cut the next sheet.
59. As the sheets are done, remove the excess cardstock, weed the butterflies, and bend them in half to get an open wing effect.

60. Place two glue dots on each butterfly and tape them from the glitter ribbon to flow down and up around the sides of the bigger butterfly.
61. Open a new project in Design Space.
62. Select 'Text' from the menu on the left-hand side.
63. Type "Live Be," unlock the text and set the size to fit.
64. Choose the font you like for the wall decal. This project uses 'A Perfect Day' font as an example.
65. Set the font size you want depending on how tall and wide you want the font to be on the wall.
66. Change the text color to gold (to be cut on the gold removable vinyl).
67. Duplicate the font.
68. Change the text to "Life Free."
69. Change the text color to dark red (to be cut on the wine removable vinyl).
70. The slogan will be "Live Life Be Free." "Live" and "Be" will be printed in gold, while "Life" and "Free" will be printed in wine.
71. Click 'Make it.'
72. Use the removable vinyl to cut the letters.
73. When the letters have been cut and weeded, transfer them onto the wall using transfer tape into the position you desire.

CONCLUSION

We all know that a Cricut is a work of art and that the press is the heart of the machine. Presses are special projects and powerful tools in their own right, and they deserve recognition as such. To help you recognize your press as an artistic piece, we've found a number of ways to decorate your kitchen or any room for that matter.

These are the most popular ways to decorate your press, but we're sure there's something additional we're missing!

As we end this book, let's take a look at some of the benefits of using CRICUT press components.

(A) True to the Cricut Logo – This is the main reason I bought the Cricut press components because they are so consistent with the Cricut logo. I know that all of my designs will be just as unique as the ones that were made by the original Cricut designer.

(B) More Versatile – The fact that I don't have to order expensive vinyl singles anymore means that I am free to make many different designs using slightly different parts. The best part is, I don't have to order them separately like I did with my Vinyl 2 machines!

(C) Affordable – This machine does not come cheap, but it is by far much more bang for your buck than buying individual vinyl parts just so that you can make your own designs. You'll find that you can make just about any design you want using CRICUT press components!

Decorating Your Press

Here are our top ways to decorate your Cricut press.

1. Wood panels: Cricut wood panels are also great for creating unique patterns on your kitchen table, mantle or dining area. You can cut shapes from wood panels and trace them onto cardstock to create elaborate designs. Make patterns with different colors of your favorite papers and tape them onto wood panels for even more detail.

2. Mini Cricut: Smaller versions of Cricuts can be used as door stops, scrapbooking tools or on shelves by simply taping them onto black foam board.

3. Stencils: Stencils are rather similar to wood pieces but are made of paper instead. They come in all sorts of sizes, shapes and patterns, so there's bound to be something you like! Stencils can be used on doors, walls, shelves or on furniture, giving them quite an interesting appearance.

4. Pillow Covers: Cricut pillow covers can be used for anything from gift cards to wall art for a touch of whimsy in any room of your home. Simply cover the back of each pillow with decorative fabric and attach photos or designs with double-sided tape (we recommend using Gluestick). Thread some ribbon through them and you have instant decorative pillows!

The Cricut is a tool for hobbyists, crafters, and woodworkers alike. It is used for cutting shapes out of wood and other materials. But with so many amazing attachments for this tool, it can also be used in many other ways. In fact, I am sure that you have heard about some of its special features.

One of the most useful features of the Cricut is how it can be customized to make your projects your own. You can add or remove different parts from the press to make it fit your needs perfectly. With this amazing feature, it is possible to make custom-made projects for all your friends and family!

Another cool feature of the Cricut is how you can use it to cut patterns out of vinyl, paper, or fabric. You can cut out any design you want to create using this incredible tool.

If you are interested in using the Cricut design software, then check out these tips! The Cricut software is easy to use and will help your complete projects with no problems! The software will allow you to easily design designs, edit them, and even duplicate your previous design again or something completely different!

If you are interested in making projects that are personal and unique, then pick up a Cricut today! They are durable tools that will last longer than anything else! Once you start using one, there is no way that you will want to stop! All these amazing features and unique design tools will allow you to make pieces that no one else has ever seen before!

Lightning Source UK Ltd.
Milton Keynes UK
UKHW020634190121
377315UK00013B/1142